Hardik Gohel

Human Brain Computer Interface (H-BCI)

Hardik Gohel

Human Brain Computer Interface (H-BCI)

LAP LAMBERT Academic Publishing

Cover image: www.ingimage.com

Publisher:
LAP LAMBERT Academic Publishing
is a trademark of
Dodo Books Indian Ocean Ltd. and OmniScriptum S.R.L publishing group

120 High Road, East Finchley, London, N2 9ED, United Kingdom
Str. Armeneasca 28/1, office 1, Chisinau MD-2012, Republic of Moldova, Europe
Managing Directors: Ieva Konstantinova, Victoria Ursu
info@omniscriptum.com

ISBN: 978-3-659-77990-9

Human Brain-Computer Interface (H-BCI)

ontents

ABSTRACT ABOUT BOOK

Brain–computer interface (BCI), sometimes called a direct neural interface or a brain–machi interface (BMI), is a direct communication pathway between the brain and an external devi BCIs are often aimed at assisting, augmenting or repairing human cognitive or sensory-mot functions.

Brain-Machine Interfaces (BMI) or Brain-Computer Interfaces (BCI), also referred to as Neu Prostheses, are conceived as technological interfaces between a machine (usually a computer) a the brain of a user. They should permit the use to perform a certain task, usually witho implementing any motor action. This implies that neural impulses generated by the user's bra are detected, elaborated and utilized by the machine, just about in real-time, to perform defin tasks. As an example, information can be processed and employed to control mechanical syste (e.g. actuators) or electrical devices (e.g. electronic equipment).

A great demand for brain-machine interfaces is arising nowadays, pushed by several promisi scientific and technological recent results, which are encouraging the concentration of efforts such a direction. The possibility of measuring, processing and decoding brain activity, so that interpret neuronal signals, is regarded as the challenging possibility of bypassing broken neu and/or motor structures in patients affected by motor disorders and paralyses.

A great deal of efforts in neuroscience, robotics, and computer science are today spent by ma research groups to develop BCI. In order to provide a glance at this vast field.

This topic overview provides the communication channel between the brain signal a controlling machines, doing communication, and relevant task of brain signal.

Basically the idea for BCI to provide such a communication device through which user can eas talk, make video conference, send massages, controlling directional devices through just bra signal.

Once upon time in cognitive neuroscience and brain imaging technologies have started to prov us with the ability to interface directly with the human brain. This ability is made possi rough the use of sensors that can monitor some of the physical processes that occur within the rain that correspond with certain forms of thought.

this book, studied technologies to brain-computer interfaces (BCIs), it is explicitly anipulating brain activity instead of using motor movements to produce signals that cannot be ed to control computer or communication devices. Generally As a part of Artificial Intelligence is difficult to understand Computer Brain Interface. In existing research study there is no oper way to identify the basic concept through the applications. This leads us to specialized udy of Controlling Computer Systems by Applying Computer Brain Interface with different plications.

this Research Study Book, included History of Computer Brain Interface, Neural Control terfaces, Brain Computer Interfaces, Methods of Reading the brain – Neuroimaging in BCIs, pplications for Brain-Human Interfaces, Strategy to enhancing Human-Computer interaction th input from Active and passive Brain-Computer Interfaces.

ywords:-

gnitive Neuroscience, Brain Computer Interfaces,Brain machine interface ,Neural Control, uman-Computer Interaction,signal processing,

Chapter 1:- Introduction to Brain-Human Interface and history of BCI.

1.1 WHAT IS BCI ...?

A brain–computer interface (BCI), sometimes called a direct neural interface or a brain–machine interface, is a direct communication pathway between a brain and an external device. BCIs are often aimed at assisting, augmenting or repairing human cognitive or sensory-motor functions.

A BCI is a communication and control system that does not depend in any way on the brain's normal neuromuscular output channels. The user's intent is conveyed by brain signals (such as EEG signals) rather than by peripheral nerves and muscles, and these brain signals do not depend for their generation on neuromuscular activity. (Thus, e.g., a device that uses visual evoked potentials to determine eye-gaze direction is not a true BCI, for it relies on neuromuscular control of eye position, and simply uses the EEG as a measure of that position.)

1.2 HISTORY

Electrical signals produced by brain activity were first recorded from the cortical surface in animals b Richard Caton in 1875 (Caton, 1875) and from the human scalp by Hans Berger in 1929 (Berger, 1929).In the 75 years since Berger's first report,The history of Brain-Computer-Interfaces (BCI) start with Hans Berger's discovery of the electrical activity of human brain and the development of electroencephalograpy (EEG).

Pic: 1.1 : Hans Berger   Pic :1.2 : Berger's patient

erger studied medicine at the University of Jena and received his doctorate in 1897. He became a
ofessor in 1906 and the director of the University's psychiatry and neurology clinic in 1919. In 1924
erger was the first one who recorded an EEG from a human brain.

y analyzing EEGs Berger was able to identify different waves or rhythms which are present in a
ain, as the Alpha Wave (8 – 12 Hz), also known as Berger's Wave.Berger's first recording device was
ry rudimentary. He inserted silver wires under the scalp of his patients. Those were replaced by
lber foils which were attached to the patients head by rubber bandages later on. Berger connected
ese sensors to a Lippmann Capillary Electrometer, with disappointing results.

ore sophisticated measuring devices such as the Siemens double-coil recording galvanometer, which
splayed electric voltages as small as one ten thousandth of a volt, led to a success.berger analyzed the
terrelation of alternations in his EEG wave diagrams with brain diseases.EEGs permitted completely
w possibilities for the research of human brain activities. However, it took until 1970 before the first
velopment steps were taken to use brain activities for simple communication systems.

ie Advanced Research Project Agency (ARPA) of the government of the United State of America
came interested in this field of research. They had the vision of increasing the performance of mental
gh load tasks by enhancing human abilities with artificial computer power. However these ambitious
als were never fulfilled but the first steps into the right direction were taken.

ectroencephalographic (EEG) activity has been used mainly for clinical diagnosis and for exploring
ain function. Nevertheless, throughout this period, scientists and others have speculated that the EEG
other measures of brain activity might serve an entirely different purpose, that they might provide
e brain with another means of conveying messages and commands to the external world. While
rmal communication and control necessarily depend on peripheral nerves and muscles, brain signals
ch as the EEG suggested the possibility of non-muscular communication and control, achieved
ough a brain–computer interface (BCI).

Research on BCIs began in the 1970s at the University of California Los Angeles (UCLA) under a grant from the National Science Foundation, followed by a contract from DARPA. The papers published after this research also mark the first appearance of the expression brain–computer interface in scientific literature.It has been known since the pioneering work of Hans Berger more than 80 years ago that the brain's electrical activity can be recorded noninvasively through electrodes on the surface of the scalp. Berger observed that a rhythm of about 10Hz was prominent on the posterior scalp and reactive to light. He called it the alpha rhythm. This and other observations showed the electroencephalogram (EEG) could serve as an index of the gross state of the brain. Despite Berger's careful work many scientists were initially skeptical, with some suggesting that the EEG might represent some sort of artifact. However, subsequent work demonstrated conclusively that the EEG is indeed produced by brain activity.

the field of BCI has since blossomed spectacularly, mostly toward neuroprosthetics applications that aim at restoring damaged hearing, sight and movement. Thanks to the remarkable cortical plasticity of the brain, signals from implanted rostheses can, after adaptation, be handled by the brain like natural sensor or effector channels. Following years of animal experimentation, the first neuroprosthetic devices implanted in humans appeared in the mid-nineties.

hapter 2:- Concept of Dissertation and Existing Study work

concept of dissertation

uch popular speculation and some scientific endeavors have been based on the fallacious assumption at BCIs are essentially "wire-tapping" or "mind-reading" technology, devices for listening in on the ain, detecting its intent, and then accomplishing that intent directly rather than through muscles.This sconception ignores the central feature of the brain's interactions with the external world:that the otor behaviors that achieve a person's intent, whether it be to walk in a certain direction,speak certain rds, or play a certain piece on the piano, are acquired and maintained by initial and continuing *aptive changes* in CNS(central nervous system) function.

ring early development and throughout later life, CNS neurons and synapses continually change th to acquire new behaviors and to maintain those already acquired (Salmoni et al., 1984; Ghez and akauer, 2000). Such CNS plasticity underlies acquisition of standard skills such as locomotion and eech and more specialized skills as well, and it responds to and is guided by the results achieved. For ample, as muscle strengths, limb lengths, and body weight change with growth and aging, the CNS justs its outputs so as to maintain the desired results.

is Research paper is about to controlling devices through brain like directional devices, virtual lity games, communication media such as message passing, operating computers and mobile nmunications as well.

re by, the above researches I want to give my own idea about how a BCI can operate wireless vices i.e. mobile, communication media and some extent of the computer operation with brain nals.

. Early work :

e is some of the experiments which was research by the different scientist and researcher s. on ferent animals ,patients, and for different aspects.

2.2.1. Research on Monkey

As almost all experiments which include a certain risk for human lives, the first experiments we conducted with animals more precisely on primates. Work groups led by Schmidt, Fetz and Bak found out that monkeys could get control over the firerate of individual neurons in the primary mot cortex, which is responsible for executing voluntary movements after a short period of training time.

The first wireless intracortial brain-computer interface was build by Philip Kennedy and his colleagu by implanting neurotrophic cone electrodes into monkey brains. Several research groups worked on t real-time reconstruction of more complex motor parameters using recordings from neural ensembl which are clusters of neurons performing a particular neural computation. However, the research brain-computer-interfaces made only little progress during its first years, but approximately 10 yea ago an explosive development in this field started. Miguel Nicolelis, a Brazilian physicist and scient became the most popular proponent of using multi area recordings from neural ensembles as input BCI applications, as these recordings provide a very high quality. In the 90s Nicolelis team did ini studies on rats,followed by the development of a BCI system that was able to decode monkeys' bra activities. This data was used to translate the monkeys' movement to rudimentary robot action.

By the year 2000, Nicolelis' group implanted electrode arrays into multiple brain areas of owl monke They built a BCI system that was capable of reproducing a monkey's movement, while reaching food or using a joystick in real time. However, the system has to be considered as an open-loop BCI, the monkeys got no feedback from their actions by the BCI.

They proceeded with their research and conducted experiments in rhesus monkeys. The monkeys w trained to reach and grasp for objects on a screen by manipulating a joystick. Using velocity a grasping action prediction their BCI system was able to control a robot. The robot was hidden from monkey but the monkey was provided with feedback of the robot's performance by the visual display

Pic.: 2.1. : Miguel Nicolelis

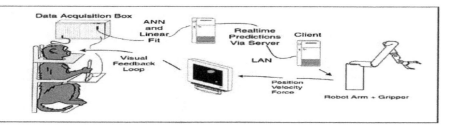

Fig:-2.1 :- Nicolelis monkey experiment

g says:- Behavioral setup and control loops, consisting of the data acquisition system, the computer nning multiple linear models in real time, the robot arm equipped with a gripper, and the visual splay. Robot position was translated into cursor position on the screen, and feedback of the gripping rce was provided by changing the cursor size.

2.2 research on Humans

owever, not only monkeys were objects to BCI research but also humans participated in experiments th both invasive (which means direct contact to the neurons by whatever means) and non-invasive proaches.

There have been many experiments using various techniques for "reading the brain" such as the EEG MEG, fMRI or similar methods. Some BCI designs rely on a phenomenon called "Cortial Plasticity" which states that the location of certain processing functions in the brain can change as the result experience. This means that this type of design relies heavily on the user adapting to the BCI in order make it function correctly. From a Human-Computer Interface point of view this is not an acceptable solution. Rather one would expect the BCI to adapt to the user for increased usability.

This approach has been implemented and has proven to be quite successful One of the first person who benefit from all the years of BCI research is **Matt Nagle**. In 2004 an electrode array w implanted into his brain to restore functionalities he had lost due to paralysis.The system required som training but finally he was able to control the TV,check emails and do basically everything that can achieved by using a mouse.He could also open and close a prosthetic hand.

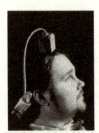

Pic:2.2 : Matt Nagle

Today many researchers at a lot of universities and laboratories are continuing BCI research.Howeve the present-days achievments are very impressive but there is still a lot of research and studying to done until the whole potential of Brain-Computer-Interfaces can be tapped.

2.2.3. Mobile Telephony

Some of the most cutting-edge interfaces — technologies that even go beyond gestural interfaces li Microsoft's **Kinect** — might be much closer to implementation than you think.In fact, a group researchers in San Diego have developed a system that allows users to dial a phone number on cellphone using only their thoughts. The method is surprisingly accurate and would be a hu dvantage for people with disabilities or anyone who needs a more hands-free experience or who gularly performs tasks that require a high degree of mental focus.

he technology, which was **developed** by University of California, San Diego neuroscience searcher **Tzyy-Ping Jung** and colleagues, tracks electrical activity in the brain using a headband of ectrodes and a **Bluetooth** device. Users of the system were shown digits from zero to nine flashing at ightly different speeds on a computer screen; the frequency of each digit was detected by the ectrodes, allowing the Bluetooth device to "know" which numbers to dial.

various trials, subjects with varying degrees of training showed between 70% and 85% accuracy hen attempting to dial a 10-digit phone number.Computer-brain interfaces have been around for a hile; this is the first instance we've seen of a brain interface being applied to a mobile phone. Being le to make brain interfaces smaller, faster and cheaper might go a long way toward these novel chnologies becoming more practical for everyday use for a mass audience.

2.4. Other Research work

ere are also some other research like , on rat for moving arms for the cheese from cave In addition w a days scientist and developer also try to develop some of the application like controlling some of e system through brain like televisions, games, controlling devices in such a way that human brain n handle these things through brain signals.

A brain–computer interface allows paralyzed patients to play music with brainpower alone.

Pic :2.3:The brain-computer interface allows paralyzed patients to play music just by thinking about it.*ICCMR Research Team - University of Plymouth*

A pianist plays a series of notes, and the woman echoes them on a computerized music system. Th woman then goes on to play a simple improvised melody over a looped backing track. It doesn't sou like much of a musical challenge — except that the woman is paralyzed after a stroke, and can ma only eye, facial and slight head movements. She is making the music purely by thinking.

This is a trial of a computer-music system that interacts directly with the user's brain, by picking up t tiny electrical impulses of neurons. The device, developed by composer and computer-music speciali Eduardo Miranda of the University of Plymouth, UK, working with computer scientists at t University of Essex, should eventually help people with severe physical disabilities, caused by brain spinal-cord injuries, for example, to make music for recreational or therapeutic purposes. The findin are published online in the journal *Music and Medicine*."This is an interesting avenue, and might very useful for patients," says Rainer Goebel, a neuroscientist at Maastricht University in t Netherlands who works on brain-computer interfacing.

hapter 3:- Study Computer Brain Interface and its applications

1. Study of BCI.

1st century is a great era of technological implementation of brain computer technology within all a of science, business, gaming, research.

this chapter we discus about how brain control the different communication devices. Like text nversion,communication,device controls from the brain signals and what is the success ratio and ferent aspects.

There are several reasons why BCI is an important and active research area:

- BCI is a new neuroscience paradigm that might help us better understand how the human brain works in terms of plasticity and reorganization, learning, memory, attention, thinking, social interaction, motivation, interconnectivity, and much more.

- predict user intentions (such as movement planning) swiftly and reliably

- take appropriate actions (control a device, give neuro feedback to a user).

- BCI research allows us to develop a new class of bioengineering control devices and robots to provide daily life assistance to handicapped and elderly people.

- BCI can expand possibilities for advanced human computer interfaces (HCIs), making them more natural, flexible, efficient, secure, and user-friendly by enhancing the interaction between the brain, the eyes, the body, and a robot or a computer.

- transform this data into reliable information then knowledge;

- provide easy-to-use neurofeedback by effective visualization and sonification of the extract brain signals as well as a graphical interface to display or visually confirm this knowledge.

3.2 .Types of BCI.

BCI work on the base of two types of technologies which are…

1. *Non - invasive:*
   Without penetrating thes kalp, mostly EEG, rarely magneto encephalogram (MEG)

2. *Invasive:*
   Implanted sensors (electrode array, needle electrodes,electrocorticogram (ECoG)

3.2.1. Non invasive BCI :

"Brain cap" technology being developed at the University of Maryland allows users to turn th thoughts into motion.

Design and operation of a BCI system Electrophysiological signals reflecting brain activity a acquired from the scalp, from the cortical surface, or from within the brain and are processed measure specific signal features (such as amplitudes of evoked potentials or EEG rhythms or firi rates of single neurons) that reflect the user's intent. These features are translated into commands t operate a device, such as a word-processing program, a wheelchair, or a neuroprosthesis.

It is Independent from peripheral nerves and muscles, using only central nervous system (CN activity. Users can voluntarily produce the required signals The system detects when the user wants emit a command that means it is asynchronous.

Pic: 3.1:-The user has a EEG cap on. By thinking about left and right hand movement the user controls the virtual keyboard with her brain activity.

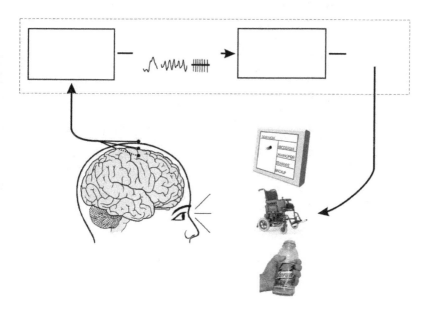

Fig 3.1: basic BCI overview.

3.2.2. Invasive BCI

It is basically dependent on peripheral (non - CNS) –activity.e.g., controlled eye - Movement. Evoked Potentials: Users modulate brain responses to external stimuli (automatic or voluntarily).

Invasive BCI is purely based on chip where a small kind of chip can b placed at some of the physical part of body from where user can not work properly like robotic hand.

A small chip is implanted at the physical layer or inside the body at muscle, sensory or internal level for capturing the sense signals for the controlling the device likewise operating the connected device with the body.

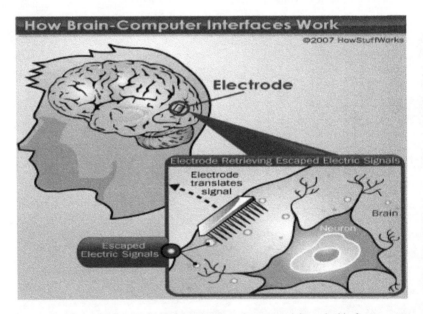

FIG 3.2.:- invasive BCI :- where signal can be captured through chip from neurons.

ep 1:- chip is placed to a particular physical area
ep 2:- chip capturing the signal.
ep 3:- signal analysis.
ep 4:- accordingly device control(like robotic arm, pace maker etc).

this type of BMIs the signals originated by brain are recorded by implanted electrodes. Because of
s invasivity, the applicability of this approach is limited to animal experiments. Development of this
stem has two basic directions: improvement of both implantable electrodes and signal processing
ethods.

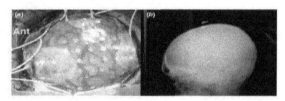

C:3.2..: Examples of electrode placement and ECoG signals. (a) Intra-operative placement of a 64-
ectrode subdural array. Inter-electrode spacing was 1 cm and electrode diameter was 2 mm; Ant:
terior. (b) Post-operative lateral skull radiograph showing grid placement

Chapter 4:- Signal processing.

Process:-

A BCI records brain signals and processes them to produce device commands. This signal processing has two stages. The first stage is feature extraction, the calculation of the values of specific features of the signals. These features may be relatively simple measures such as amplitudes or latencies of specific potentials (e.g., P300), amplitudes, or frequencies of specific rhythms (e.g., sensorimotor rhythms), or firing rates of individual cortical neurons, or they may be more complex measures such as spectral coherences. To support effective BCI performance, the feature-extraction stage of signal processing must focus on features that encode the user's intent, and it must extract those features as accurately as possible.

The second stage is a translation algorithm that translates these features into device commands. Features such as rhythm amplitudes or neuronal firing rates are translated into commands that specify outputs such as cursor movements, icon selection, or prosthesis operation. Translation algorithms may be simple (e.g., linear equations), or more complex (e.g., neural networks, support vector machines)(Mülleret, 2003).

To be effective, a translation algorithm must ensure that the user's range of control of the chosen features allows selection of the full range of device commands. For example, suppose that the feature the amplitude of a 8–12 Hz mu rhythm in the EEG over sensorimotor cortex; that the user can vary the feature over a range of 2–10_V; and that the application is vertical cursor movement. In this case, the translation algorithm must ensure that the 2–10_V range allows the user to move the cursor both up and down. Furthermore, the algorithm must accommodate spontaneous variations in the user's range control (e.g., if diurnal change, fatigue, or another factor changes the available voltage range) (e.g., Ramoser et al., 1997). Finally the translation algorithm should have the capacity to at least accommodate, and at best encourage, improvements in the user's control. For example, if the user range of control improves from 2–10 to 1–15_V, the translation algorithm should take advantage this improvement to increase the speed and/or precision of cursor movement control. This need continual adaptation of the translation algorithm to accommodate spontaneous and other changes in the gnal features is in accord with the fundamental principle of BCI operation (i.e., the continuing pendence on system/user and user/system adaptation), and has important implications. First, it means at new algorithms cannot be adequately evaluated simply by offline analyses. They must also be ted online, so that the effects of their adaptive interactions with the user can be assessed. This testing ould be long term as well as short term, for important adaptive interactions may develop gradually. cond, the need for continual adaptation means that simpler algorithms, for which adaptation is ually easier and more effective, have an inherent advantage. Simple algorithms (e.g., linear uations) should be abandoned for complex alternatives (e.g., neural networks) only when online as ell as offline evaluations clearly show that the complex alternatives provide superior performance.

. Signal processing steps:-

any efforts have been carried out in order to implement effective control algorithms based on the ocessing of EMG signals. Starting from the first attempts in the late 1940s, several EMG-based orithms have been developed and used to enhance the functionality with different devices.

e formal scheme for the acquisition and analysis of the EMG signal for the control of prosthetic vices is composed of several modules:-

❏ signal conditioning and preprocessing
┐ eature extraction
Dimensionality reduction
attern recognition
Offline and online learning

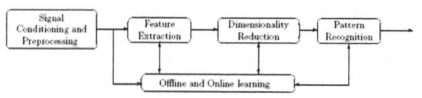

FIG 4.1..: Scheme for acquisition and analysis of an EMG signal

Signal processing analysis is a tedious task to analyse signal in proper way by different algorithms.
we seen in above figure that different steps for recognize the functions which is important and selecti
of nature of signals.

Here is some of the signal processing activities define in the next picture....

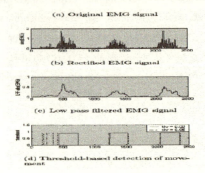

(a) Original EMG signal

(b) Rectified EMG signal

(c) Low pass filtered EMG signal

(d) Threshold-based detection of movement

hapter 5:- Neural Control Interfaces and its applications

xperiments in humans utilizing modern invasive and non-invasive brain imaging technologies as terfaces have been conducted. The most commonly studied potential interface for humans has been ectroencephalography (EEG), mainly due to its fine temporal resolution, ease of use, portability, and st of set-up. However practical use of EEG as a BCI requires a great deal of user training and is ghly susceptible to noise. In 2004 scientists of the Fraunhofer Society utilized neural networks to ift the learning phase from the user to the computer and thus recorded noticeable results within 30 inutes of training. Magneto encephalography (MEG) and even functional magnetic resonance aging (fMRI) have both been used successfully as rudimentary BCIs, in the latter case allowing two ers being scanned in real-time to play Pong against one another by altering their hemodynamic sponse through various biofeedback techniques.

Recent studies have shown that imagining the execution of a particular sensori-motor task gives e to almost the same pattern of neuronal activity in central nervous system as actual performance of e sensori-motor task. The state of the art is that correct decoding of EEG signal is possible to a very 'ge extent. It is still not good enough for applications since the erroneous responses in a remaining % can lead to completely wrong actions. The main challenge in BCIs EEG-based is to identify the rticular EEG signal components (features) that can be successfully used as control commands

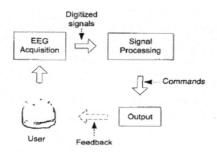

FIG :5.1.:-General BCI architecture

The main, but not unique, problem in these approaches is that single trial EEG data is very noisy, with data stemming from many sources. The characteristic responses to specific events are usually obtained by averaging signals from many trials, like in evoked signals. To successfully match single trial data the relevant source of the signal needs to be separated out before it can be matched to average templates.

In matching, a similarity measure is applied to compare the signal trial with each template. The measure is still easily distorted by signals from non-relevant parts of frequency spectrum. After matching, a vector of similarity measurements for the different channels and the different templates needs to be classified into a category judgment. Optimal methods need to be found that do not over-fit data.

A rating of confidence of the judgment is much needed as outputting a wrong symbol may have a high cost in some situations. This aspect is lacking in all procedures proposed in literature so far. The system should work only in regions of high confidence.

EEG electrodes may bring many practical problems, like sensitivity to electromagnetic radiation, difficulty to place and position, varying conductance, usually a limited number of channels, and discomfort when used for a longer time.

There are few new concepts in the design of EEG measurement systems like miniaturized, battery powered front-end close to patient, with fiber optic data transfer to the signal processing PC (see [7],[14]), or use of active electrodes, which have the property that the first amplifier stage is integrated within the electrode.

A group of the most important authors in the field of non-invasive BCIs gave the list of goals important for future progresses of these systems [15]. Future progress will depend on:

1) identification of those signals, whether evoked potentials, spontaneous rhythms, or neuron firing rates, that users are best able to control;
2) development of training methods for helping users to gain and maintain that control;
3) delineation of the best algorithms for translating these signals into device commands;

4) attention to elimination of artefacts as electro-myographic and electro-oculographic activity;

5) adoption of precise and objective procedures for evaluating BCI performance.

: Graz University, the group of Pfurtscheller is one of the leading groups in Europe. They have tensive experience in recording and analyzing EEG signals with the aim to use them to restore nctionality in patients who lost the ability to move their limbs (tetraplegia). They are also doing basic search, focusing on beta and gamma synchronization of cortical EEG activity. These oscillations in e frequency range between 15 and 70 Hz provide information about attention for perception and tion. But the signal-to-noise ration in this frequency range is not high enough to use these signals for iable on-line control. Their ultimate work is aimed at assessing the feasibility of walking through a tual city by using motor imagery. Therefore they combined EEG based BCI with Virtual Reality R) technology.

BCI transforms bioelectrical brain gnals, modulated by mental activity g. imagination of hand movement) into control signal. This signal is used to lk forward/backward or remain stationary inside a virtual city . ey demonstrated that the combination a BCI with VR as a feedback means

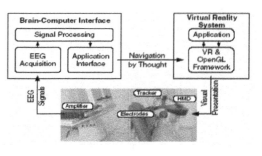

ms a feasible system for navigation in very simple virtual environments.

FIG:5.2.: Schematic model of a combined framework, where the BCI system consists of the EEG *input, extracts and classifies EEG-parameters and calculates a control signal, which is sent to the V* *system and influences there the visual feedback.*

5.1. APPLICATIONS

5.1.1 Medical applications

BCIs provide a new and possibly only communication channel for people suffering from seve physical disabilities but having intact cognitive functions. For example these devices could help treating (or rather overcoming) paraplegia or amyotrophia.Somewhat related to this topic is the field Neuroprosthetics which deals with constructing and surgically implanting devices used for replaci damaged areas of the brain and more generally for neural damages of any kind. For example, the mo widespread neuroprosthetic (approx. 85,000 people worldwide 2005) is the cochlear implant or bion ear. This device can help people with impaired hearing. In contrast to conventional hearing aids th device is not a sound amplifier but directly stimulates any appropriate functioning nerves.

5.1.2. Aerospace application

One of the most important aerospace fields of applications is devoted to interfacing a human arm with powered exoskeleton (orthotic device). As an example, such a type of system was implemented in elbow joint, The Human–Machine interface was set at the neuromuscular level, by using neuromuscular signal (EMG) as the primary command signal for the exoskeleton. The EMG sigr along with the joint kinematics were fed into a myoprocessor, which in turn predicted the musc moments on the elbow joint. An exoskeleton is an external structural mechanism whose join correspond to those of the human body. It is worn by the human and the physical contact between t operator and the exoskeleton allows direct transfer of mechanical power and information signals.

5.1.3. virtual reality

irtual reality is a one of the up growing technology in the field of gaming, training applications like ace pilot training etc. thest is a signal generation and analysis from past feedback can be use to ntrol that brain computer interface system for virtual reality.

.4. mental state monitoring.

nducting all the signal trials from patient brain and different pattern analysis different mental state n be monitored via different brain signal techniques for future reference and treatment from pattern alysis.

Chapter 6:- Methods of Reading the Brain –Neuroimaging in BCIs

Reading the brain : -

6.1 what is Neuroimaging ?

"Neuroimaging includes the use of various techniques to either directly or indirectly image the structure, function, or pharmacology of the brain. It is a relatively new discipline within medicine and neuroscience."

6.2 TYPES OF NEUROIMAGING TECHNIQUES

6.2.1 Direct Neural Contact

This is the most accurate method of recording potentials occurring in the brain as it has direct contact every neuron in the brain, e.g. by using nano robots. Needless to say that this method is highly invasi and impracticable with respect to our current technology. However, with ongoing advances nanotechnology this method might become reality.

6.2.2 Electroencephalography (EEG).

Experiments in humans utilizing modern invasive and non-invasive brain imaging technologies interfaces have been conducted. The most commonly studied potential interface for humans has be electroencephalography (EEG).

This procedure is the first non-invasive neuroimaging technique discovered. It measures the electri activity of the brain. Due to its ease of use, cost and high temporal resolution this method is the m widely used one in BCIs nowadays. However, in practice EEGs are highly susceptible to noise and t quire a significant amount of user training in order to be operable in a BCI. Luckily, recent research the Fraunhofer Society [WIKI_BCI] has shown that this problem can be overcome by using neural tworks to shift the learning overhead from the human to the computer.

2.3. Magnetoencephalography (MEG).

hough similar to the EEG in that it is a non-evasive technology the MEG is a much newer and more curate technology. Instead of measuring the electrical activity in the brain this technology records agnetic fields produced by it. The main drawbacks of this technology are its high requirements in uipment.

Using MEG requires a room filled with super-conducting magnets and giant super-cooling helium nks surrounded by shielded walls."

2.4. Functional Magnetic Resonance Imaging (fMRI).

is technique measures the haemodynamic response (blood flow and blood oxygenation) related to ural activity in the brain by the use of MRI (Magnetic Resonance Imaging formerly known as agnetic Resonance Tomography MRT). The fact that there is a correlation between neural activity d the brain's haemodynamics makes the fMRI a neuroimaging tool. In contrast to the MRI which dies the brain's structure this method studies the brain's function. As this method requires MRI chnology it needs very special equipment and thus is quite costly.

2.4.1. Direct Interfaces via EEG.

Pic 6.1. :- Test person attached to an EEG

In the field of Body-Computer-Interfaces multiple approaches to an interface design have evolve Many of these are in fact haptic or linguistic interfaces. But for some people who experienced cerebral apoplexy and are "locked-in", trapped in their own body so to say, the operation of tho devices is impossible. Therefore, a different technique – the direct communication with the brain via electro-encephalogram (EEG) is applied here. In the following four different techniques an application examples are presented and compared subsequently.

6.2.4.2. VEP-Interface:-

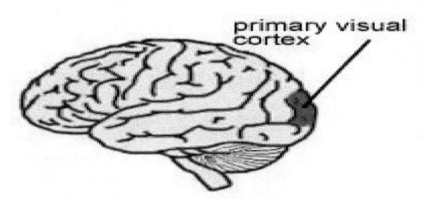

FIG 6.1. : Location of the visual cortex

VEP stands for visual evoked potential which is caused by a visual stimulation. When a person exposed to commonly-used visual stimuli like flashing lights or flickering checker boards, significa changes in the EEG of the visual cortex can be observed.

or measuring an EEG, multiple electrodes have to be attached to the subject's back of the head over e visual cortex as well as two electrodes r reference and grounding. When hich changes its colors from black to equency of between 3 and 6 Hz the n be measured via the electrodes.

on an earlap and on the brow exposed to a checkerboard white and back with a visual system emits a VEP that

FIG:6.2. : Example of a VEP-based user interface.

classical application of the VEP-technique is the "Brain Response Interface" developed by Erich E. tter in 1992 . Although this is one of the first application examples it still has a remarkable rformance in the face of speed. Sutter's experiment consists of a checkerboard with 64 boxes. easurements show that the EEGs have different characteristics with each field the subject focused. tter put the letters of an alphabet and some frequently-used English words into the 64 boxes and corded all 64 EEGs for each box/symbol. During operation a computer program compares the current Gs with those in the database and then assembles words and sentences together.

e problem with this experiment is that it requires the subject to permanently concentrate on the reen which can be very exhausting, especially when it flickers. This can be quite easily solved by roducing a simple on/off switch in one of the boxes.

other experiment was designed by Pieter J. Cilliers and Andre J.W. Van der Kouwe in 2000 . stead of presenting a matrix of letters on the screen a keyboard is displayed. Each of the four rows of ys have a different color. In the four corners of the screen they put flickering LEDs in the rresponding colors. When the computer program registers a significant change in the EEG – so if the subject concentrates on one of the LEDs – it replaces the picture on the screen by another one which only shows the focussed row of keys. This is now again split into four blocks associated with a unique color, etc. The process is repeated until the desired letter is selected. So it requires three steps to select letter. By reducing the number of possible signals from 64 to 4 the precision and thus the performance could be increased. With an average speed of 15 seconds per letter this is a quite respectable speed. Another idea of optimization is to make frequently used letters faster to access by reordering the key by applying the Huffman code on the English language e. g.

6.2.4.3..P300-Interface

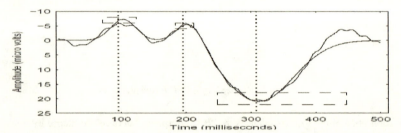

FIG:6.3. : Graph of a P300 signal, significant amplitude increase after 300ms.

P300 is a term for a significant positive curve on the EEG which appears 300ms after a relevant a seldom stimulation that does not necessarily have to be visual. The strongest signal can be obtained the central parietal region which is located at the upper back of the head. This signal occu involuntarily so no special training is required. Research has shown that stimuli with an erotic conte lead to stronger P300 brain waves. Another study found out that P300 signals were weaker in tobacc smokers, alcoholics and drug-dependent people. Nevertheless, a P300 characterizes a stimulus which perceived by the subject as eminent.

Dr. Larry Farwell and Emanual Donchin made use of the P300 and developed a typing tool that w made up of a matrix of 6 x 6 fields containing letters of the alphabet. To find out what letter the subj wants to type the program first highlights all six columns then the six rows consecutively. The progra

:asures the P300 according to each highlighted column and row and finds out the strongest signal. On ⅰs way the desired letter can be identified. Unfortunately, the error rate of this device initially was ⅰte high. Still with a speed of around 2.3 letters per minute this is   an acceptable

2.4.4. ERS/ERD - Interface : -

Pic:6.2.: *Patient using the*
Combined ERS/D
& FES technology to
grasp a glass method.

e event related synchronization / de-synchronization is a signal type that can be measured when the ɔject imagines a hand or foot movement. ERS / ERD was researched by a team at the technical ⅰversity of Graz in Austria [CA_EEG]. They also developed an interface which allows movement of ⅰursor in a two dimensional space by combining hand and foot movement. After two training sessions ɛe of the five test persons achieved a success rate between 89 and 100 percent, the two other persons ⅼy 51 and 60 percent. This could have the cause in different imaginations of hand movement each ʳson has After a 62 training sessions with 160 trials a 25-year old paraplegic patient could move the ʳsor practically error-free. Regarding his immense handicap the accomplishment of 0.95 letters per ⅼute is definitely respectable. Another experiment was done at the technical university Graz. They ⅰbined the ERS/ERD Interface with a FES (functional electrical stimulation) which is the ⅰulation of muscles using surface electrodes. A patient who had lost his ability to grasp with his ⅰd is now no longer impeded.

6.2.4.5. SSVE P- Interface:-

SSVEP stands for steady *state visual evoked potential*. This occurs when focusing on a flickering ne
tube. It is a series of VEPs which is observed as steady amplitude on the EEG. The signal can
amplified using biofeedback which is nothing else than showing the subject current measurements.
properly trained the subject is able to increase or lower this amplitude and thus can trigger events if t
amplitude goes above or below a certain threshold. The American research team around Matthew
Middendorf developed a flight simulator that turned the plane to the right if the amplitude went ove
threshold and to the left if below [BCIT_TP]. After an average of 6 hours per test person the succe
rate lay around 80 percent.Middendorf also experimented with a 2D cursor control using four LE
flickering in distinct frequencies. The advantage of this method is that no biotraining is required as t
subject does not have to control the amplitude of the SSVEPs. He or she only has to concentrate on c
of the four LEDs to move the cursor up/down or left/right. It took 2.1 seconds in average for each LI
with a success rate of 92 percent. The clear disadvantage is the extremely exhausting flickering
lights which also represents a hazard for epileptics.

Comparison :-

System	Training duration	Letters per minute	Error rate
VEP	10 – 60 min	30	10%
P300	5 min	4	5%
ERS/ERD	2 – 3 h	1	< 11%
SSVEP	6 h	--	< 20%

Table 6.1: *Listing and characterization of the four technologies*

CONCLUSION:-

Depending on the use case each technology has its pros and cons, but when wanting to type letters V
is still the fastest and most efficient method. In the case of more analogue control ERS/ERD is m
applicable. Of course, there are many more techniques and application scenarios than shown in t
paper, but these somehow show the basics. These can be combined in order to increase precision a
functionality.

ıture applications will probably leverage a more detailed picture of brain waves and there is also a ɛnd towards implants so that very specific signals can be filtered. Also, implants are of good use if the ɜG is too weak – e. g. as a result of a cerebral apoplexy.

Chapter 7:- Brain Computer Interface for mobile devices

7.1.Introduction:-

Brain-computer interface (BCI) systems acquire electroencephalography (EEG) signals from t
human brain and translate them into digital commands which can be recognized and processed on
computer or computers using advanced algorithms .BCIs can provide a new interface for the use
suffering from motor disabilities to control assistive devices such as wheelchairs. Over the past tw
decades, different features of EEG signals such as mu/beta rhythms, event-related P300 potentials, a
visual evoked potentials (VEP) have been used in BCI studies. Among these different BCI regimes, t
VEP-based BCI has obtained increasing attention due to its advantages including high informati
transfer rate (ITR), little user training, low user variation, and ease of use.Steady-state visual evok
potential (SSVEP) is the electrical response of the brain to the flickering visual stimulus at a repetiti
rate higher than 6 Hz . The SSVEP is characterized by an increase in amplitude at the stimul
frequency, which makes it possible to detect the stimulus frequency based on the measurement
SSVEPs.

The frequency coding approach has been widely used in SSVEP-based BCI systems .In such a syste
each visual target is flickering at a different frequency. The system can recognize the gaze target of t
user by detecting the dominant frequency of the SSVEP. Although robustness of the syste
performance has been demonstrated in many laboratory studies, moving this BCI system from
laboratory demonstration to real-life applications still poses severe challenges to the BCI communit
To design a practical BCI system, the following issues need to be addressed: (1) ease of use,
reliable system performance, (3) low-cost hardware and software. Recently, with advances in t
biomedical sciences and electronic technologies, the development of a mobile and online BCI has be
put on the agenda . In real-life applications, BCI systems should not use a bulky, wired El
acquisition device and signal processing platform .

Using these devices will not only uncomfortable and inconvenient for the users, but will also aff
their ability to perform routine tasks in real life. Furthermore, signal processing of BCI systems sho

in real-time instead of off-line analysis. Several studies have demonstrated the use of portable vices for BCIs. Lin et al. proposed a portable BCI system that can acquire and analyze EEG signals ith a custom DSP module for real-time monitoring. Shyu et al. proposed a system to combine an EG acquisition circuit with an FPGA-based real-time signal processer. To the best of our knowledge, cellphone- based online BCI platform has not been reported.This study aimed to integrate a wearable d wireless EEG system with a mobile phone to implement an SSVEP-based BCI. The system nsists of a four-channel biosignal acquisition/amplification module, a wireless transmission module, d a Bluetooth-enabled cell-phone. This study also demonstrates its implications in a case study in hich wearers' EEG signals were used to directly make a phone call. Realtime data processing was plemented and carried out on a regular cell-phone. In a normal office environment, an average formation transfer rate (ITR) of 28.47 bits/min was obtained from ten healthy subjects.

e envision that many mobile applications can be reinvented; for example, instead of hand dialing ur friend while driving you can simply wink or think of him while your phone displays your ntacts. We envision that wireless EEG headsets will become cheaper and more robust and that achine learning techniques developed for high end research-grade wired EEG headsets can be fectively exploited by resource limited phones. As this vision gathers speed and noise issues are ved, EEG will be integrated into wearable fabric (e.g., baseball caps, woolen hats, bicycle helmets) become the new wireless "earphones plus" (i.e., earphones plus a limited set of electrodes).This ses a number of interesting issues. For example,the NeuroPhone system relay (discussed later) nsmits raw unencrypted neural signals over-the-air to the iPhone in IP packets. This leads to the tion of insecure "neural packets everywhere," opening up important privacy challenges that need to addressed.

Methods

.1 System Hardware Diagram

typical VEP-based BCI that uses frequency coding consists of three parts: visual stimulator, EEG cording device, and signal processing unit [2]. The basic scheme of the proposed mobile and wireless BCI system is shown in Fig. 1. The hardware of this system consists mainly of three maj-components: a stimulator, an EEG acquisition unit and a mobile cell-phone.The visual stimulat- comprises a 21-inch CRT monitor (140Hz refresh rate 800x600 screen resolution) with a 4 x 3 stimul matrix constituting a virtual telephone keypad which includes digits 0-9, BACKSPACE and ENTE The stimulus frequencies ranged from 9Hz to 11.75Hz with an interval of 0.25Hz between tw consecutive digits. The stimulus program was developed in Microsoft Visual C++ using the Microsc DirectX 9.0 framework.

Fig. System diagram of mobile and wireless BCI

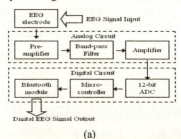

(a)

(b)

Fig. (a) Block diagram of the EEG acquisition unit, (b) an EEG headband with an embedded data acquisition and wireless telemetry unit.

The EEG acquisition unit is a 4-channel wearable bio-signal acquisition unit. Fig.(a) shows the da flow of EEG acquisition unit . EEG signals were amplified (8,000x) by instrumentation amplifie Band-pass filtered (0.01-50 Hz), and digitized by analog-to-digital converters (ADC) with a 12- resolution. To reduce the number of wires for high-density recordings, the power, clocks, and measur signals were daisy-chained from one node to another with bit-serial outputs. That is, adjacent nod ectrodes) are connected together to (1) share the power, reference voltage, and ADC clocks, and (2) isy-chain the digital outputs. Next, TI MSP430 was used as a controller to digitize EEG signals using DC via serial peripheral interface with a sampling rate of 128Hz. The digitized EEG signals were en transmitted to a data receiver such as a cell-phone via a Bluetooth module. In this study, Bluetooth odule BM0203 was used. The whole circuit was integrated into a headband (Fig. 2(b)). The ecifications of the EEG acquisition unit are listed in Table. Data processing unit was realized using a okia N97 (Nokia Inc.) cell-phone. A J2ME program developed in Borland JBuilder2005 and Wireless velopment Kit 2.2 were installed to perform online procedures including (1) displaying EEG signals time-domain or frequency-domain on the screen, (2) band-pass filtering, (3) estimating power ectrum of the VEP using fast Fourier transform (FFT), (4) presenting auditory feedback to the user, d (5) phone dialing. The resolution of the 3.5-in touch screen of the phone is 640 x 360 pixels.

.2.Wireless EEG Headset:-

e use the Emotiv EPOC headset which has 14 datacollecting electrodes and 2 reference electrodes. e electrodes are placed in roughly the international 10-20 system and are labeled as such . The adset transmits encrypted data wirelessly to a Windowsbased machine; the wireless chip is prietary and operates in the same frequency range as 802.11 (2.4Ghz). The software that comes with Emotiv headset provides the following detection functionality: various facial expressions (referred as "Expressiv" by Emotiv); levels of engagement, frustration, meditation, and excitement Affectiv");subject-specific training and detection of certain cognitive neuro-activities such as "push", ull", "rotate", and "lift" ("Cognitiv") . Also built in the headset is a gyroscope that detects the change orientation of subject's head. The headset is not meant to be an extremely reliable device, thus it is illenging to extract finer P300 signals from the EEGs this headset produces. But, as we state in our ion, this headset can be easily deployed at large scale because of its low price, and can be extremely dy if we can extract useful signals (e.g., P300) from it through smart signal processing and ssification algorithms running on the phone.

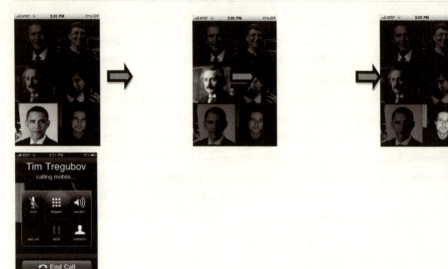

Fig:- ("The Dial Tim") application works on similar principles to P300-speller brain-compu
interfaces: the phone flashes a sequence of photos of contacts from the address book and a P300 neu
signal is elicited when the flashed photo matches the person whom the user wishes to dial. EEG sign
from the headset are transmitted wirelessly to an iPhone, which natively runs a simple classifier
discriminate P300 signals from noise. When a person's contact-photo triggers a P300, their pho
number is automatically dialed. In this case, the user wants to dial Tim, thus when his picture
flashed, Tim is automatically
dialed.

Table 1. Specification of EEG acquisition unit

Type	Example
Channel Number	4
System Voltage	3V
Gain	8,000
Bandwidth	0.01~50 Hz
ADC Resolution	12bits
Output Current	29.5mA
Battery	Lithium 3.7V 450mAh 15~33hr
Full Scale Input Range	577μV
Sampling	128Hz
Input Impedance	greater than 10MΩ
Common Mode Rejection Ratio	77dB
System Voltage	88dB
Gain	18mm x 20mm, 25mm x 40mm

2.3. System Software Design

hen the program is launched, the connection to the EEG acquisition unit would be automatically tablished in a few seconds. The EEG raw data are transferred, plotted, and updated every second on e screen. Since the sampling rate is 128 Hz, the screen displays about 4-sec of data at any given time. g. 3(a) shows a snapshot of the screen of the cell-phone while it was plotting the raw EEG data in the 1e-domain. Users can switch the way of displaying from time-domain to frequency-domain by essing the "shift" + "0" button at the same time. Under the frequency-domain display mode, the wer spectral density of each channel will be plotted on the screen and updated every second, as own in Fig. 3(b). An auditory and visual feedback would be presented to the user once the dominant quency of the SSVEP is detected by the program. For example, when number 1 was detected by the stem, the digit "1" would be shown at the bottom of the screen and "ONE" would be said at the same 1e.

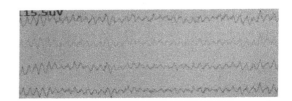

(a)

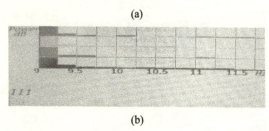

(b)

Fig.. Screen snapshots of the cell-phone's GUI: (a) A time-domain display of the 4-channel EEG, (b) Estimated power spectral density of the EEG when number '1' was attended.

Fig. shows the flow chart of the program. First, the program initiates a connection to the EE acquisition unit. Next, four-channel raw EEG data are band-pass filtered at 8-20 Hz, and then plott on the screen every second. The display can be switched to the power spectrum display mode pressing "shift" + "0" buttons simultaneously,as shown in Fig. A 512-point FFT is applied to the EE data using a 4-sec. moving window advancing at 1-sec. steps for each channel. To improve t reliability,a target is detected only when the same dominant frequency is detected in two consecuti windows (at time k, and k+1 seconds, k≥4). The subjects are instructed to shift their gaze to the ne target (digit) flashed on the screen once they are cued by the auditory feedback.

7.2.4. BCI Experiment Design

Ten volunteers with normal or corrected to normal vision participated in this experiment.T experiment was run in a typical office room. Subjects were seated in a comfortable chair at a distan of about 60 cm to the screen. Four electrodes on the EEG headband were placed around the O1/(area, all referred to a forehead midline electrode.At the beginning of the experiment, each subject w asked to gaze at some specific digits to confirm the wireless connection between the EEG headba and the cell-phone. Based on the power spectra of the EEG data, the channel with the highest signal- noise ratio was selected for online target detection. The test session began after a couple of sh practice session. The task was to input a 10-digit phone number:123 456 7890, followed by an ENT key to dial the number. Incorrect key detection could be removed by a gaze shift to

BACKSPACE" key. The percentage accuracy and ITR were used to evaluate the performance of the cell-phone based BCI.

.-T. Wang, Y. Wang , and T.-P. Jung
g.

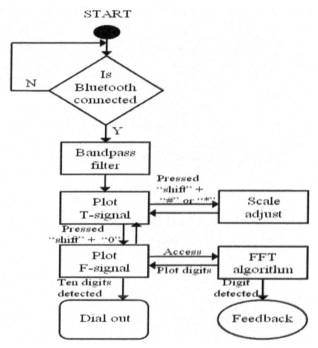

The flow chart of the program coded on the cell-phone. T-signal refers to the timedomain display, and F-signal refers to the frequency-domain display.

2.5. EEG base mobile implementation.

this section, we discuss the implementation details of the wink mode and the think mode for the Dial n application.

Due to the fact that the headset only transmits encrypted data wirelessly and this data can be decrypte solely by Emotiv's closed-source SDK on a Windows machine, we use a laptop to relay the raw EE data to the phone through WiFi. Upon receiving the EEG data, the phone carries out all the releva signal processing and classification. The headset samples all channels at 128 samples/second, each which is a 4-byte floating-point numbercorresponding to the voltage of a single electrode. The data ra of the EEG data streamed from the relay laptop to the mobile phone is 4kbps per channel. For ea application mode, only relevant channels are streamed. The phone uses simple machine learnin techniques to determine user input (wink/non-wink or P300/non-P300). For the wink mode, we rever mount the headset and only use the channels which are directly above the subject's eyes, i.e., O1 a O2. We develop a data collection program where the subject can easily label each wink. A multivaria Bayesian classifier is then trained and used for classification. We set equal-prior such that it will not biased toward either wink or non-wink classes. In the preprocessing step, we calculate variances over 90% overlapping sliding window of the two channels.

The variances are used as features and are fed to the classifier in the classification stage. During t offline training phase, 2D Gaussian distributions are estimated for both the wink and non-wink class, illustrated in Figure 8. The two Gaussians are mostly separated, which results in good onli classification performance. For the think mode of the application, which utilizes the P300 signal, v attempt to use similar 2D Gaussians. However,the distributions of the classes prove to be t overlapped for reasonable classification. As discussed in the design consideration section, to cancel c unnecessary noise we preprocess the data by filtering it with a 0-9Hz bandpass filter and averaging t signal over multiple trials. We do this preprocessing separately for all 6 stimuli corresponding to the images of the Dial Tim application. Following this we only crop the signal segment that corresponds the highest peak value at around 300ms after the stimulus onset. For classification, we use a decisi stump whose threshold is set to the maximum value among the cropped signal segments for all images.

7.2.6. Design consideration.

what follows, we discuss a number of design considerations that relate to building a reliable and bust Neuro-Phone system.

gnal to Noise Ratio (SNR): Since the Emotiv headset is not intended for finer signal detection, there more noise than usual on every electrode of the EEG. To compound this issue, EEG's are relatively isy to begin with Assuming that this noise is relatively random, it has the potential to completely validate the data that we use to detect winks and P300 signals in the first place. We study various lutions to increase the SNR, such as bandpass fil-tering and independent component analysis (ICA) 4].A sensible approach to increase the SNR is to average the data over many trials, which is also a mmonly used technique neuroscience [10]. Naturally, this introduces delay in the acquisition of a reliable P300 signal, cause we need to average several trials before actually detecting the P300. However, in wink mode can avoid averaging because wink signals are much more easily detectable in raw EEG data than 00 signals.

gnal Processing: Although we are averaging data for a better SNR, we can still improve the EEG nals for better P300 detection. We use a bandpass filter to get rid of any noise that is not in the P300 quency range [14]. Again this signal processing is unnecessary for wink mode because wink signals much more easily detectable in raw EEG data.

one Classifiers: Typically, realtime EEG signal processing and classification algorithms are signed for powerful machines, not resource limited mobile phones. For example ,use a weighted nbination of various classifiers for EEG classification. These classification algorithms are not ictical to run on the mobile phone because of power efficiency and resource issues. To address this illenge, we combine two approaches for efficient classification on the phone: i) we do not supply all innels from the headset to the phone for classification, rather, only the relevant subset of EEG innels; and ii) we implement lightweight classifiers, more specifically, a multivariate equal-prior yesian classifier is used for wink mode and a simple decision stump is used for the think mode.

7.2.7. Evaluation and Results.

To evaluate our system, we test the wink and think modes in a variety of scenarios (e.g., sittir walking) using two different Emotiv headsets and three different subjects. In what follows, we discu our initial results.For the wink mode, we collect multiple sessions of data from all subjects while th sit relaxed or walk, then train an equal-prior Bayesian classifier using a set of five sessions of data fro a single subject sitting relaxed. This classifier is then applied to the rest of the data to test whether can generalize to unseen data by calculating the classification precision (i.e., percentage of classifi "winks" that are actuallyreal winks), recall (i.e., percentage of real winks that are actually classified winks) and accuracy (i.e., percentage of all events that are correctly classified). The experiment resu are shown in Table 1. As can be seen from the table, the classifier performs well on data collected : sitting-relaxed scenarios but walking results in a decline in performance. The decline of recall sugge that while the subjects are walking, a small amount of blinks are contaminated such that the classif fails to pick them up; thus,representing false negatives. There is a larger decline in precision, wh suggests that in additional to the increase in false negatives reflected by the recall, there is also increase in false positives; noisy peaks in EEG data caused by walking are erroneously picked up the classifier as blinks. Despite the performance decline of the wink classifier when applied to mo noisy data, we can, however, still observe that it is robust in reasonably noisy scenarios.

	Sitting Relaxed	Walking
Precision	92.35%	86.15%
Recall	99.39%	96.70%
Accuracy	95.58%	92.58%

Table 1.1.: Wink classification results

For think mode, we test on the same set of subjects. We carry out the P300 experiments with subjects using the application while sitting still, sitting with loud background music, and standing We average the data over a set time interval. The accuracy values of the experiments are shown Table . First, the accuracy increases as the data accumulation time increases, which coincides with intuition that averaging over more data improves the SNR for the expected P300 signals, leading higher accuracy. Second, P300 signals are quite susceptible to external noise, illustrated by the fact t hen subjects are sitting still, we have the best accuracies, whereas accuracy decreases when nsiderable auditory noise is introduced.accuracy further declines when the subjects stand up, which tentially adds more noise due to subjects' muscle controls and physical movements. Finally, even ough different experiment settings result in different P300 detection accuracies, more data cumulation and averaging generally yields better detection accuracies.

Time	Sitting	Music (Sitting)	Standing
20s	77.78%	44.44%	33.33%
50s	77.82%	66.67%	66.67%
100s	88.89%	88.89%	66.67%

ble 1.2. : Think classification accuracies. Times in the first column indicate the different time rations of data accumulation for averaging. Contact pictures are flashed once every half a second in idom order; each of the 6 pictures has a 1/6 chance for each flash. Accuracy measures the proportion correctly classified sessions. Note that chance levelclassification accuracy would be 1/6 " 16.67%.

Table 2. shows the results of the EEG-based phone-dialing experiments. All subjects completed EEG-based phone-dialing task with an average accuracy of 95.9±7.4%,

Table 2. Online test results of 10 subjects

Subject	Input length	Time(sec.)	Accuracy (%)	ITR
Y.T.	11	72	100	32.86
C.	11	72	100	32.86
A.	19	164	78.9	14.67
Y.B.	11	73	100	32.4
T.P.	17	131	82.4	17.6
T.	11	67	100	35.31
W.	11	72	100	32.86
B.	13	93	92.3	20.41
F.	11	79	100	29.95
D.	11	66	100	35.85
Mean	12.6	88.9	95.9	28.47

and an average time of 88.9 seconds. 7 subjects successfully inputted 11 targets without any error. Th average ITR was 28.47±7.8 bits/min, which was comparable to other VEP BCIs implemented on high-end personal computer.

7.2.8. Conclusions and Discussion

This study detailed the design, development, and testing of a truly mobile and wireless BCI f communication in daily life. A lightweight, battery-powered, and wireless EEG headband was used acquire and transmit EEG data of unconstrained subjects in real-world environments. The acquir EEG data were received by a regular cellphone through Bluetooth. Signal-processing algorithms a graphic-user interface were developed and tested to make a phone call based on the SSVEPs responses to frequency-encoded visual stimuli. The results of this study concluded that all of t participants, with no or little practicing, could make phone calls through this SSVEPbased BCI syste in a natural environment.Despite such successes, there is room for improvement. Future directio include:

(1) the use of dry EEG electrodes over the scalp locations covered with hairs to avoid skin preparati and the use of conductive gels; and

(2) the use of multi-channel EEG signals to enhance the accuracy and ITR of the BCI, as oppos to manually selecting a single channel from the recordings.

We have presented the evaluation of an initial prototype that brings together neural signals and phor to drive mobile applications in new ways. One could argue that connecting the wireless Emotiv EPC EEG headset and iPhone is just a simple engineering exercise. We believe the NeuroPhone system is important development precisely because it is simple to engineer using cheap but noisy commerc components. NeuroPhone opens up new opportunities and challenges in ubiquitous sensing a pervasive computing. For example, sniffing packets could take on a very new meaning if brain-mob phone interfaces become widely used. Anyone could simply sniff the packets out of the air a potentially reconstruct the "thoughts" of the user. Spying on a user and detecting something as simp them thinking yes or no could have profound effects. Thus, securing brain signals over the air is an important challenge.

is worth noting that, in the current study, the cell-phone was programmed to assess wearers' SSVEPs r making a phone call, but it can actually be programmed to function in ways appropriate for other CI applications. In essence, this study is just a demonstration of a cell-phone based platform chnology that can enable and/or facilitate numerous BCI applications in real-world environments.

FIG:-an EEG base phone architecture

Fig:- A user using EEG base application on Iphone.(neurophone)

Chapter 8:- Strategy to enhancing Human-Computer Interaction via BCIs.

8.1 Human enhancement:-

"Human enhancement describes any attempt (whether temporary or permanent) to overcome th current limitations of human cognitive and physical abilities, whether through natural or artifici means."

Having this definition in mind one can think of many applications of the BCI in this field. For examp BCIs could help facilitate communication systems in Cybernetic Organisms, Brainwa Synchronization, or even speculative things such as the Exo-cortex, among others.

Cybernetic Organism describes the enhancement of an organism by means of technology. For examp a BCI could enable the attachment of robotic limbs without the use of the organism's original nervo system (as long as the brain is intact).

8.2 Brainwave Synchronization

"Brainwave synchronization is the practice to entrain one's brainwaves to a desired frequency, I means of a periodic stimulus with corresponding frequency. The stimulus can be aural as in the case binaural beats, or visual, as with a Dreamachine."

A BCI could be used to detect and classify the current state of mind of an individual and actively adji the frequency of the Brainwave Synchronization to achieve a certain state of mind.

8.3 Excortex

"An exocortex (speculative) is an external information processing system that augments, in a subtle a seamless fashion via a brain-computer interface, the brain's biological high-level cognitive processes.

8.4. Human manipulation

e notion that a BCI could allow a two-way communication between a human and a computer gives
e to more controversial potential uses of such a device. Using such a communication mechanism one
uld imagine directly influencing an individual's thoughts, decisions, emotions or thinking. Of course,
e mere "reading" of the mind could be put to criminal use, e.g. unwanted reading of passwords,
cations, etc. While this may sound like science-fiction, methods researched in social-psychology such
advertisement, media manipulation, propaganda, group dynamics or peer pressure have been proven
be successful in altering an individual's behavior and their effectiveness is undisputed. So, in
inciple manipulation is possible. Experiments to explore possibilities of mind-control are by no
eans theoretical and include the use of drugs and electronic signals to alter brain functioning. For
ample the project codenamed MKULTRA conducted by the CIA dates back to the 1950's and was
med at researching mind control .Brain-computer-interfaces present a new level of technology that
uld be used to actively manipulate an individual.

5. Current Projects

 already mentioned many projects are going on in the world of BCI research.Here are some of them
esented:

5.1 Berlin Brain-Computer-Interface (BBCI)

e Berlin Brain-Computer-Interface is a joint venture of several german research organizations.
mbers are:

he Institute Computer Architecture and Software Technology of the Fraunhofer Society
The research group Intelligent Data Analysis (IDA)
The Neurophysics Research Group
The department of Neurology at the Campus Benjamin Franklin of the Charité University
Medicine
he Technical University Berlin The BBCI project is sponsored by the Ministry for Education   and
search of the German government.

The goal of the project is the development of an EEG based BCI system. The applications of this system are on the one hand computer supported workplaces, to control a cursor via brain waves and the other hand tools for paralyzed or paraplegic people.The BBCI project aims to shift the ma learning effort to the computer. Therefore robust artificial learning and signal processing algorithm need to be developed to classify and interpret the brain waves correctly.

8.5.2. Graz Brain-Computer-Interface

The University of Graz, Austria has also a research project for Brain-Computer-Interfaces.Its ma topics are:

– Brain-Computer-Interfaces :-Using EEG signals as input for computers.
– Telemonitoring of BCIs:-Remote monitoring and administration of BCI systems
– Combining BCI and virtual reality (VR) technology Using BCI systems to move in virtual   realitie
– Functional electrical stimulation: Stimulation of limbs by electrical signals
The Graz Brain-Computer-Interface project partner of several international research projects as:
– Presenccia (European Union)
– Eye2It (European Union)
– Direct Brain Interface (National Institute of Health, USA)

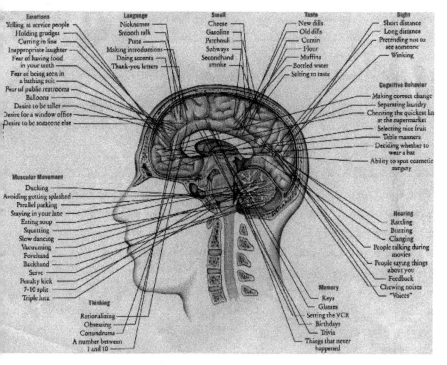

FIG :- brain sensory.

5. Future work :-

ere is a limited amount of related work in this area. A number of groups use research/professional-
ality EEG devices that offer higher quality signals but are expensive and based on wired headsets. In
ntrast, consumeroriented EEG headsets are considerably cheaper and noisier, but at the same time
: more geared toward gaming applications rather than the types of classification we have used them
'. Typically, these headsets are wireless, enabling mobile uses. are more closely related to
uroPhone. develops a wireless EEG headband prototype with 4 electrodes targeting non-hairy skin
:a of the forehead, which is not suitable for P300 detection. is a commercially available headset with

a single electrode not powerful enough for the types of applications we have in mind such as Dial Tir
These projects connect neural signals to mobile phones just to display visualization and simp
frequency-domain analysis of the signal, not to drive mobile applications themselves. In essence, t
phone is used as a mobile display and not as a phone.

8.7. Conclusion:-

We have presented the evaluation of an initial prototype that brings together neural signals and phon
to drive mobile applications in new ways. One could argue that connecting the wireless Emotiv EPC
EEG headset and iPhone is just a simple engineering exercise. We believe the NeuroPhone system is
important development precisely because it is simple to engineer using cheap but noisy commerc
components. NeuroPhone opens up new opportunities and challenges in ubiquitous sensing a
pervasive computing.For example, sniffing packets could take on a very new meaning if brain-mob
phone interfaces become widely used. Anyone could simply sniff the packets out of the air a
potentially reconstruct the "thoughts" of the user. Spying on a user and detecting something as simp
as them thinking yes or no could have profound effects. Thus, securing brain signals over the air is
important challenge.

[1] F. Lotte, M. Congedo, A. L´ecuyer, F. Lamarche, and B. Arnaldi. A review of classification algorithms for EEG-based brain-computer interfaces. J Neural Eng, 4(2):R1–R13, Jun 2007.

[2] A. Mouraux and G. Iannetti. Across-trial averaging of event-related EEG responses and beyond. Magnetic resonance imaging, 26(7):1041–1054, 2008.

[3] K. Li, R. Sankar, Y. Arbel, and E. Donchin. P300 Based Single Trial Independent Component Analysis on EEG Signal. Foundations of Augmented Cognition.Neuroergonomics and Operational Neuroscien pages 404–410, 2009.

[4] A. Mouraux and G. Iannetti. Across-trial averaging of event-related EEG responses and beyond. Magnetic resonance imaging, 26(7):1041–1054, 2008.

[5] Cen, D., et al., "Advances in neural interfaces: report from the 2006 NIH Neural Interfaces Workshop, " J. Neural Eng. 4, S137 (2007)

[6] Kostov, A. and Polak, M. (2000). Parallel man-machine training in development of EEG-based cursor control. IEEE TransRehabil Eng, 8, 203–205.

[7] Wolpaw, J.R., McFarland, D.J., Vaughan, T.M. and Schalk, G.(2003). The Wadsworth center brain– computer interface research and development program. IEEE Trans Neural SysRehabil Eng, 11, 204–207.

■ The Brain Machine Interface: Alan S. RudolphDEC 2001 DSO (.ppt)

■ *Brain-Computer Interface* ttp://www.nanoaging.com/wiki/Brain-computer_interface
Last modified: 03:29, 26 September 2005 24.54.174.32

0] *Human Enhancement* http://en.wikipedia.org/wiki/Human_enhancement
Last modified: 04:02, 22 April 2006 Mr. Billion

1] Andrew T. Campbell, Tanzeem Choudhury, Shaohan Hu, Hong Lu, Matthew K. Mukerjee▪ , Mashfiqui Rabbi, and ▪jeev D. S. Raizada (August 30, 2010) 'NeuroPhone: Brain-Mobile Phone Interface using a Wireless EEG Headset

2] Jonathan R. Wolpawa,b,*, Niels Birbaumerc,d, Dennis J. McFarlanda , Gert Pfurtschellere , Theresa M. Vaughan March 2002) 'Brain–computer interfaces for communication and control', *Clinical Neurophysiology 113 (2002), (),* ▪. 767-791

3] Vrushali R Pavitrakar (2013) 'Survey of Brain Computer Interaction', *International Journal of Advanced Research Electrical, Electronics and Instrumentation Engineering* , 2(4), pp. 1647-1652.

4] *Berlin Brain-Computer-Interface* http://bbci.de/

5] *Graz Brain-Computer-Interface* http://bci.tugraz.at/index.html

3] *Clinical application of an EEG-based brain-computer interface: a case study*in a patient with severe motor impairment Authors: Neuper C, Müller G, Kübler A,Birbaumer N, Pfurtscheller G.Clinical Neurophysiology, 114(3):399-409 (2003).

▼]*Brain-Computer Interface* http://www.nanoaging.com/wiki/Brain-computer_interface
Last modified: 03:29, 26 September 2005 24.54.174.32]

▪] *A VEP-based Computer Interface for C2-Quadriplegics* Authors: Cilliers, P.J. & Van Der Kouwe, A.J.W., 1993

▪] *Brain-computer interfaces based on the steady-state visual-evoked response* Authors: Middendorf, M.S., McMillan, G., Calhoun, G., und Jones, K.S.,1999 Brain-Computer Interface Technology: Theory and Practice:First International Meeting Program and Papers, The Rensselaerville Institute,Rensselaerville, New York, pp. 78—82, June 16-20, 1999.

▪] *Brainwave Synchronization* http://en.wikipedia.org/wiki/Brainwave_synchronization
Last modified: 19:57, 28 April 2006 Army1987

] *Matt Nagle* http://en.wikipedia.org/wiki/Matt_Nagle
Last modified: 05:00, 12 April 2006

▪] *Hans Berger* http://en.wikipedia.org/wiki/Hans_Berger
Last modified: 20:15, 16 April 2006

▪] Gohel, Hardik. "Nanotechnology Its future, Ethics & Challenges." In *National Level Seminar - Tech* ▪mposia on IT Futura, p. 13. Anand Institute of Information & Science, 2009.

▪] Gohel, Hardik, and Dr. Priti Sajja. "Development of Specialized Operators for Traveling Salesman Problem ▪P) in Evolutionary computing." In *Souvenir of National Seminar on Current Trends in ICT(CTICT 2009)*, p. GDCST, V.V.Nagar, 2009.

[25] Gohel, Hardik, and Donna Parikh. "Development of the New Knowledge Based Management Model for E-Governance." *SWARNIM GUJARAT MANAGEMENT CONCLAVE* (2010).

[26] Gohel, Hardik. "Interactive Computer Games as an Emerging Application of Human-Level Artificial Intelligence." In *National Conference on Information Technology & Business Intelligence*. Indore 2010, 2010.

[27] Gohel, Hardik. "Deliberation of Specialized Model of Knowledge Management Approach with Multi Agent System." In *National Conference on Emerging Trends in Information & Communication Technology*. MEFGI, Rajkot, 2013.

[28] Hardik Gohel, Vivek Gondalia. "Accomplishment of Ad-Hoc Networking in Assorted Vicinity." In *National Conference on Emerging Trends in Inf ormation & Communication Technology (NCETICT-2013)*. MEFGI, Rajkot, 2013.

[29] Gohel, Hardik, and Disha H. Parekh. "Soft Computing Technology- an Impending Solution Classifying Optimization Problems." *International Journal on Computer Applications & Management* 3 (2012): 6-1.

[30] Gohel, Hardik, Disha H. Parekh, and M. P. Singh. "Implementing Cloud Computing on Virtual Machines an Switching Technology." *RS Journal of Publication* (2011).

[31] Gohel, Hardik, and Vivek Gondalia. "Executive Information Advancement of Knowledge Based Decision Support System for Organization of United Kingdom." (2013).

[32] GOHEL, HARDIK, and ALPANA UPADHYAY. "Reinforcement of Knowledge Grid Multi-Agent Model for e-Governance Inventiveness in India." *Academic Journal* 53.3 (2012): 232.

[33] Gohel, Hardik. "Computational Intelligence: Study of Specialized Methodologies of Soft Computing in Bioinformatics." *Souvenir National Conference on Emerging Trends in Information & Technology & Manageme (NET-ITM-2011)*. Christ Eminent College, Campus-2, Indore, 2011.

[34] Gohel, Hardik, and Merry Dedania. "Evolution Computing Approach by Applying Genetic Algorithm." *Souvenir National Conference on Emerging Trends in Information & Technology & Management (NET-ITM-2011)*. Christ Eminent College, Campus-2, Indore, 2011.

[35] Gohel, Hardik, and Bhargavi Goswami. "Intelligent Tutorial Supported Case Based Reasoning E-Learning Systems." *Souvenir National Conference on Emerging Trends in Information & Technology & Management (NET-ITM-2011)*. Christ Eminent College, Campus-2, Indore, 2011.

[36] Gohel, Hardik. "Deliberation of Specialized Model of Knowledge Management Approach with Multi Agent System." *National Conference on Emerging Trends in Information & Communication Technology*. MEFGI, Rajkot, 2013.

[37] Gohel, Hardik. "Role of Machine Translation for Multilingual Social Media." *CSI Communications - Knowledge Digest for IT Community* (2015): 35-38.

[38] Hardik, Gohel. "Design of Intelligent web based Social Media for Data Personalization." *International Jour of Innovative and Emerging Research in Engineering(IJIERE)* 2.1 (2015): 42-45.

[39] Hardik, Gohel. "Design and Development of Combined Algorithm computing Technique to enhance Web Security." *International Journal of Innovative and Emerging Research in Engineering(IJIERE)* 2.1 (2015): 76-7

[40] Gohel, Hardik, and Priyanka Sharma. "Study of Quantum Computing with Significance of Machine Learning." *CSI Communications - Knowledge Digest for IT Community* 38.11 (2015): 21-23.

1] Gondalia, Hardik Gohel & Vivek. "Role of SMAC Technologies in E-Governance Agility." *CSI ommunications - Knowledge Digest for IT Community* 38.7 (2014): 7-9.

2] Gohel, Hardik. "Looking Back at the Evolution of the Internet." *CSI Communications - Knowledge Digest for Community* 38.6 (2014): 23-26.

www.ingramcontent.com/pod-product-compliance
Lightning Source LLC
LaVergne TN
LVHW042349060326
832902LV00006B/494